We Look West

Poets of the Northfield, Minnesota, Public Library

Up On Big Rock Poetry Series
SHIPWRECKT BOOKS PUBLISHING COMPANY
Winona, Minnesota

Books by Poets of the Northfield Public Library

Using the pseudonym Sadie Montgomery, **Becky Boling** has published several print and ebook novels with iUniverse Press: Sadie Montgomery's three-book "Phoenix of the Opera Series" (2007): "The Phoenix of the Opera," "Out of the Darkness: The Phantom's Journey," and "The Phantom's Opera" (2007), continued with "Phantom Death" (2008), "Phantom Madness" (2009), "Phantom Murder" (2010), and "Phantom Nightmare" (2015). Stand-alone novels include: "Love's Apprentice" (2011), "Ghost Song" (2012), and "Willoughby" (2013).

"Jumping the Median," (Encircle Publications 2019); "Catastrophizing in Catastrophe," (DEG 2023), both books by **D.E. Green**.

"Ghosting" by **Steve McCown**, (Up On Big Rock Poetry Series 2020), a Shipwreckt Books imprint.

"Relative Space," (2021); "When Life Was Still," a fictional trilogy (2020) by **Julie A. Ryan.**

We Look West

Poets of the Northfield, Minnesota, Public Library

Becky Boling
Heather Candels
D. E. Green
Steve McCown
Julie A. Ryan

Cover and interior design by Shipwreckt Books
Cover photo of downtown Northfield, Minnesota, by Becky Boling

Shipwreckt Books Publishing Company
357 W. Wabasha Street
Winona, Minnesota 55987

Library of Congress Control Number: 2024930917

In memory of our late colleague, Harold David Walters, and with gratitude to Rob Hardy, who, as Northfield Poet Laureate, brought us all together.

Contents

Introduction by Rob Hardy

Becky Boling

Heather Candels

Julie A. Ryan

Introduction by Rob Hardy

Poet Laureate of Northfield, Minnesota 2016-2023.
July 2023.

It's our cue to call it a night/ but we resist the wrap of darkness.

In the final poem of this collection, "We Look West," Julie Ryan perfectly captures the mood that pervades the work of the five poets collected here. These poets are up front about growing older and confronting their mortality, but they haven't come close to calling it a day. They have lived through some dark times—for example, a near-death experience that disappointingly didn't include an encounter with Elvis—but their poems stand as lights at the end of the tunnel. We leave Julie Ryan facing West, toward the fading sunset, but we also find D.E. Green getting up early to walk the dog, when there are still "just hints of blue and light/in the East." These poems are always looking for the light, and in all directions. There's a line in Steve McCown's poem "Homemade": "a lasting source of light." Not the sun or the stars or nuclear fusion: his grandfather's homemade ice cream. Sometimes finding the light is as simple as that.

The poems in this collection come from hearts that have been broken and mended, that have actually stopped beating and started up again. Sometimes the most profound thing we can say about life is that it goes on. We may never regain what we have lost or achieve everything we desire, but life goes on. In one of her beautiful reconstructions of a childhood experience, Becky Boling remembers the momentary thrill of being the Queen of the Monkey Bars in third grade before being humiliatingly deposed. In her virtuosic autobiographical poem "Passing," Heather Candels says of a life-changing trauma, "I got past it, at least for now." As he walks the dog, D.E. Green thinks about how he has always settled for "good enough." There is running through these poems a sense of life finding its level, of averaging out, and still being the best thing we have. In the hands of these skillful and sensitive poets, this realization is far from depressing. It's incredibly life-affirming.

In a sense, these poets, though mature in years and wisdom, are just getting started. They first came together as a group in April 2018, meeting twice monthly at the Northfield Public Library to read and comment on each other's poetry. Since then, individual members of the group have published books, appeared in the pages of literary magazines, received awards, and been nominated for the Pushcart Prize. Between Summer 2020 and Summer 2023, only one issue of *Willows Wept Review* has been without a contribution by at least one of these poets. The Summer 2022 issue of *Lost Lake Folk Opera*, a special feature on the "literary renaissance taking place today in Northfield, Minnesota," included work by all five of these poets. In June 2023, D.E. Green and Becky Boling began serving jointly as the Poets Laureate of Northfield, but each one of these poets is equally worthy of that distinction on their individual merits.

These five poets have thrived individually because they have supported each other collectively. One of the hidden currents running through this collection is their friendship. Reading this collection is like having a reunion with your five best friends from high school, catching up on each other's lives, reliving old memories, remembering other friends who are gone. Shooting hoops with Steve, listening to Julie's old mixtapes. These poems are the work of highly talented individuals, but they were created in community. Behind each poem is a conversation. You, the reader, are about to become part of that conversation.

Becky Boling

Becky Boling, the Stephen R. Lewis, Jr. Professor of Spanish and the Liberal Arts, emerita, taught at Carleton College for 36 years and has published articles on Latin American narrative and theater, creative nonfiction, dramatic monologues, short stories, and poetry. Her poems have appeared in many literary publications including *Lost Lake Folk Opera*, "Agates," "Persimmon Tree," and "Misfits."—"Tonsillectomy" and "Swept Away" appeared in *Willows Wept Review*. "Monkey Bars," "Terrarium Thoughts," and "When I'm Gone" appeared in *Visual Verse: An Anthology of Art and Words*. "Aslant" appeared in *Third Wednesday*. Northfield's SOLOS: Monologue Writing & Performance Festival performed her dramatic monologues. Twice nominated for a Pushcart Prize, her poems appear on Northfield's sidewalks, in Red Wing Arts' Poet-Artist Collaboration chapbook, as well as in the anthology, "This Was 2020." Using the pseudonym Sadie Montgomery, she's published several novels. Boling serves, along with her spouse, D. E. Green, as Northfield Interim Poets Laureate, 2023-24.

Terrarium Thoughts

I have a garden in my head.
If you opened my skull, bouquets would sprout.
I sit lotus fashion, my center of gravity
grafted to the earth, trimming, irrigating, fertilizing
wispy weedy whims that flourish
with horticultural patience into projects,
strategies, and future deeds.

I cull and harvest thoughts that render
long, scintillating monologues.
I tend random images that my fingers
doodle on scraps of paper and table tops.

I raise my arms above my head
and with tentative fingers
trace burgeoning cerebral branches,
delighting in their crinkled or smooth leaves,
curling strands of vine around my pinky,
brushing a bud's tight coils that are too new,
too naïve to risk exposure to a critical I.

From the terrarium of my skull,
green thoughts grow winsome
like the hairs on my arms and legs.
Some harden into bunions, others
remain cartilaginous like my ears and nose.
I exude universes and seed them
from my dreams with persimmon and rue.

Myopic Blessing

Was my fairy godmother
in earnest when she
saddled me
with shortness
and a sharp-edged
tongue?

> Was she a bit tipsy at the party
> when she blessed me
> with an impatient
> eye that finds
> any crack or flaw
> and can't abide
> spouting white lies
> just to be kind or polite?

Didn't she like her seat
at the banquet? Was she
too far from the festivities?
Did the potted palm
blot out her sight lines?
Is that why
I have the social grace
of a fat housefly?

> Maybe it wasn't a slight,
> or irritation,
> a poorly worded invitation,
> or a passing jibe
> that soured her mood.
> Perhaps it was just a mishap
> and she, like me, is myopic,
> her aim askew.

Or perchance,
merely circumstance
that played us both a trick.
A case of hiccups or
a fairy sneeze as she
cast the incantation?
Or did she stutter mid-speech
and out tumbled lamentation?

>Whatever her maledictions,
>intentions, or afflictions,
>she might have bequeathed
>harmony and peace
>instead of a disposition
>prone to irony and cheek.

Laughter

I once laughed at a boy
who tripped over awkward feet
he hadn't grown into yet.

I stopped when he lay too long
in the tall grass, head down.

Had my response brought him lower?

The laugh track on sitcoms I was raised on,
like sugary morning cereal,
showed me others were made of rubber,
able to fall, bounce, rebound, unscathed.

TV pratfalls performed to amuse
prepared us, from an early age,
to be both optimistic and cruel.

Tonsillectomy

our love affair was brief
after all I was
only in third grade
but when you leaned
over me—your white coat
so crisp, so clean,
with a wisp of laundry soap
and dry heat—and then
picked me up as if
our wedding cortege
had just drifted away
our vows
still hot on our lips
in sickness and in health
and now to start our lives
together, at least
for the whirlwind trip
to the gurney, where
you laid me—oh so gentle
you were, so bright
your smile, so sweet
your words—you stayed
by my side as we sped
down the aisle
and even in the cold, white room
where I knew you must leave me
even as the echo
'til death do us part
faded like your features
I sank under the mask
into dreamless sleep

Monkey Bars

Queen of the Monkey Bars, I sit,
legs dangling over a metal rod,
light beams bouncing off patent-leather shoes
across the schoolyard to blind my rivals.

I am pure balance, as at home here
above the playground as the blue jay
who mocks me from the chestnut tree
as I walk the six blocks to third grade.

Caught by the wind, my skirt balloons
like a parachute. Blue- and red-striped
polyester lashes at my face, bares thighs
and flashes my pink Tuesday panties.

Ignited by grade-school laughter,
my skin bursts into flames.
I fumble for my hem and lose
my grip on the cold, hard steel.

I fall, like Icarus, to the gravel below.
A new King of the Jungle gym
grins down at me and bellows
a Tarzan-like challenge to one and all.

Icebox

In the backyard
under the only tree we had
where my mom and grandma parked their rusty cars
there was an old icebox, squat and fat,
open door hanging askew.

My grandma had it dropped there
to make room for the new Frigidaire.
A house of women
we didn't haul large appliances
to the dump.

We didn't own a truck.

I crept to the open maw of that old icebox
left to molder and rust under a tree.
I recalled warnings of children
trapped inside. They suffocated
playing hide and seek in the city garbage dump
unable to open the door,
unable to make themselves heard.

In the shade of our dwarfed sycamore,
the appliance became a portal to a dark region,
the kind that cobwebbed dreams.
I expected to hear the moans
of the dead, to smell the sulfur
of regret as I drew near, at least
the stale reek of old cheese
and soured milk.
  I found instead a diaphanous shroud

woven of thin filaments
crisscrossing the dark
opening,
a web to ensnare
Orpheus
on his bootless return,
to punish
his lack of faith,
his impatient desire.

Before my fingers reached out
to touch the spidery veil,
the threads' vibrations
led me to the center.

There, patience itself,
the spider,
guard and keeper,
its delicate legs
strumming the strings,
enthralled me.

Grandma's Lipstick

Smoking in the dusty light of the cinema,
Grandma learned the language of make-up
from Greta Garbo and Joan Crawford.
The Majestic's grand palace, her refuge

from the factory assembly line, lured her
to the screen, long velvet drapes drawn,
fastened with golden cords worthy
of a seventeenth-century galleon in mid-sea.

In Grandma's boudoir, a delicate white vanity
fluted with gold filigree stood on curved legs
a ballerina would envy. As a child, captivated
by the fantasy of treasure, I admired her jewels—

necklaces, earrings, glass diamonds, sapphires,
rubies, fool's gold. Sniffed decanters of musky scents.
Caressed my freckled cheek with blush powder,
unsheathed cylinders of waxy color.

Dusty Rose, Russian Danger, Wild Orchid
and Femme Fatale—which did she spread
across her lips those days she headed
to the factory for an eight-hour shift?

Dusty Rose's blunt crown couldn't compete
with the slant squint of Espionage Red
or the hot fire of Night's Seduction. I
tried them all, blew kisses at the mirror.

Easter at the diner, Grandma's red lips
autographed the napkin with a Wild-Orchid
kiss. I pressed childish lips inside the moist
creamy outline and imagined a stranger's sigh.

A Mango in Mexico

summer 1974, San Luis Potosí

Flies panicked by sweetness
swarm around the vendor
as he stakes a large mango
on a stick and cuts the rind
in long voluptuous petals
away from slick orange pulp.

A month ago, a car crash,
my grandma's funeral—so
many changes, more to come.
My first trip outside the US,
summer term in Mexico
was one loss too many, so
grief was put on hold.

Fattened flies come along
with the flayed mango,
frantic to sip hot pink juice
sliding down fingers,
clinging to hand and palm.
I swat away the swarm
of buzzing gluttony.
Unrepentant, I bite into
fleshy pulp, fill
my mouth with life's
syrupy nectar.

Swept Away

That winter night, blue and frosty,
when I got into my rusty Dodge Dart
eager to spend the weekend with you,
I wasn't thinking of snow-iced roads
or blinding, glazed windowpanes
but warm laughter, hands reaching,
whispered moments on cotton pillowcases,
our complicit adolescent bodies
on the verge of adulthood—you
in your first real job, I still
in school—folding like mirror images,
one into another, the heart of sameness.

The single-lane highway threaded
west to the state line. I clutched
the wheel, fingers numb, checked
the temperature of the arctic gale
billowing from the heat vents.
Shivers along my back chipped
with an ice pick at my self-delusion.
The forced air was no warmer.

The second- or third-hand car my mother
had bought me when I turned eighteen
came without a manual, without frills,
familiar switches, levers, or dials.
Only later, when winter gave a dying roar,
would I learn how to turn on the heat.

On worn treads, I glided into the last town
my side of the border, not far from the city
where you had set up house.
I drove down a neighborhood street,
through an arboreal tunnel. Canopies
of bare branches arched and stretched
overhead, a thousand arms embraced,
despite the span of sidewalk and pavement.

Sifted snowflakes glimmered beneath
street lamps as they floated towards me,
before they could find rest on my windshield.
My headlights parted the wintery veil.
Powdery particles, far too light to resist
the gentle brush of wipers, fell
to either side of the road,
swept into the darkness.

That moment endures, a memory
that comes each winter when I drive in snow.
I watch, suspended, while snow winnows itself,
clears a path before me that still waits in patient
calm and splendor, knowing you are waiting, too.

A bower of white crystals falls, like a sacrament,
on the threshold of a life. I am already nostalgic
for what is passing, has passed, resigned
to the inevitable, but no longer able to feel the cold.

Moonwalk

Michael Jackson moonwalked
across the stage, traveling back
in time, like rewinds of Chaplin.

Daguerreotype fixed the dead,
posed them standing again
in coffins outside the mortuary.

Where did all the flowers go?
Lamentation brought home
the soldiers, maimed and dead,

sent them out again to fight.
Space changed, but blood ran

in the same direction. War
is war. All things fall apart.

Radium girls glowed, black
protestors sat on diner stools
marched across bridges,

building them, but those
bridges came down. Again.

Paradox parodies schemes
buries dreams. Reason lies

crushed by fundamentalist
belief. We stood in the light.
We thought we were safe.

A gun for every trespasser,
we no longer own our bodies.

Our streets are militarized zones,
color-coded politicized maps.

All votes are not the same.

A new century rolls belly-up
and shrinks to the 1950s. We
moonwalk, recite the Pledge
of Allegiance backward.

Violin Lesson

I shadow my son's violin lessons.
I slip into a deep cushioned armchair
behind his teacher and him. Out of sight,
I huddle in a corner of the parlor. Chintz
curtains on the large rectangular window
facing the quiet street of oak and maple
stir, like a sleeping ghost roused by music.
The only wind vibrates from bow, string,
wood as my son practices Haydn
from his Suzuki book for a summer recital.
His young teacher practices on my son, her
own children too young yet to commit
to serious study. Each arpeggio moves
me. I thrum in sympathetic vibrations, deep
and shallow breaths, my heart rises
falls, rises—his bow a conductor's baton.
I am a silent orchestra and captive audience.
Young fingers and hands graft wood
and strings to flesh. His bent arm sways,
draws geometric equations in the air.
So intense, my love, a pain I
cannot bear, cannot comprehend
as anything other than beauty.
The lesson over, my son lays
the violin, its graceful curved body,
inside the case on a cushioned bed.
Latches click in place—

this Sleeping Beauty secure
in her forest fortress. My son
looks up, ready to go.
I smile to keep my lips
from trembling.
I do not want this to end.

Wonder

I wonder if I'll lose my hair.
My mother's is sparse as if
it is being perpetually thinned
by applesauce and bingo.
She's asked for a wig
but now that an aide puts bows
in her collected locks
she's quite happy as is.

I wonder what they put in ice cream
that keeps it from melting into cold sips
the way it did when I was a kid.
Whipped it has the consistency
of marshmallow crème, the sticky stuff in a jar.
It doesn't feel right in the mouth,
doesn't refresh when swallowed.
It used to drip and stream down the throat.

Is Dairy Queen the last refuge
of the ice cream of my youth?

I wonder what a day feels like to my dog.
He gives few clues. Keeps his own counsel.

I wonder if my inner thoughts,
as I shrink into old age, will deepen
and condense into conviction. Or will they recede
like a dwarf star, hot and dense, only to explode
when I release my last breath?

Were the World to End

after Robert Browning

Who knows but the world may end tonight.
And if so, I will die only modestly old
far from the corpse that I might have become.

I have just retired to awaken to this life,
to the innocent sport of the young,
the studied patient patience of doctors,

to the struggle to be heard as who I am
rather than typecast as the aged one,
a stock role tolerated by all but the old.

Were my world to end tonight I might
rave and rage against the slight that death
so fickle would have played on me.

But, oh, the mess I would leave behind.

No tidy conclusion this, no time to write a final act.
Impossible to archive and label life's chaos.
All I have or want is time—to gather the right words,

to weave together stray threads, to find
the appropriate coda, at last to discover
my story's theme—the lesson
it might have taught.

In the Airy Space Around You

life happens. You may not
pay attention or recognize
the signs: those ghosts
are people, the muffled
poo-tee-weets*
only need translation.
The burnished and coral
brushstrokes, splashes
of cerulean and sparks
of sapphire are not
signs of a stroke, but
the world in its three
or more dimensions
flashing past you
in all their technicolor glory.
No matter where your nose
is stuck, or the averted angle
of your eyes, the wax
deposits in your ears,
in the airy space around you
what passes for life
billows and calls,
blithely flowing
a flood of scents,
sights, touch,
without you—
you, nothing
more than a boulder
in this gushing stream.

*"poo-tee-weet," Kurt Vonnegut, "Slaughterhouse 5."

When I'm Gone

Tendril me on the lattice
outside your study window.

Let me vine, cling, stretch,
rippled by your wind song,
cooled by the breath of words.

Spirit me with images—
thin tapered lines,
rounded globes,
geometric wonders.

Ivy me in arcane,
ripe, nascent words.

Tendril me in blank verse
through azure, crimson hues
with bold black strokes.

Let me sway, dip, float
on the assonance
of near rhymes,

breathe between
in the empty spaces
where thoughts pause.

Aslant

When you look at me, do it from the side.
A quick glance, from the corner of your eye
will do, better if you turn perpendicular,
your left shoulder pointed in my direction.

This slicing glimpse will catch me as I
am, that shimmer of me-ness that exists
in secret, slips around the couch edge,
over the threshold between rooms, melts

into seams of wallpaper, hides in the crack
of the door before you lean into it so it clicks
shut. I am the there that is not
there when you look at me.

Heather Candels

Heather Candels is a former English teacher and a graduate of Manhattanville College's Master of Arts and Writing program in Purchase, New York. Her work has been published in *The Prairie Home Companion Newsletter, Willows Wept Review, Inkwell, Dash, Third Wednesday, Heartlodge, The Widow's Handbook: Poetic Reflections on Grief and Survival, Lost Lake Folk Opera, Roux, and Xanadu,* among others. She was also featured in *No Small Measure,* a broadside project pairing artists and poets funded by the University of North Georgia Art Galleries.

A Sign

The hose kept knocking it down
so I yanked the sign from the lawn
and propped it
against the house.

BLACK LIVES MATTER

it announced, now unearthed,
wobbling.

Up and down the sidewalk
I saw only white
lilies of the valley
fragrant bells tinkling
in the calming breeze,
their colonies spreading underground
roots nurtured by the rich dark soil
   hidden by all it fed
still waiting for the drought to end.

Baking

She taught me
how to crack an egg.
Now she's cracking,
her yoke dispersing.

I can't contain
what's happening:
the bits —
shells first
treading in a
dripping batter,
then hiding in a souffle,
now nothing
more than a scramble,
threatening each bite
with worry.

What might we chew next?

I can't swallow this.

Brand New Key

I can almost hear the fanfare trumpets
50 years ago,
announcing the arrival of our scary new
teacher, who appeared,

– poured into a mini-dress
lips frosted, eyes eye-lined black, cat-like –

heels clacking against the warped wooden floors,
then slammed the door shut and barked s*hut up*
before she sashayed her way to the upright piano,
opened the lid and conducted us into 7th grade
music, not like our 6th grade Mr. Halvorson,
who, clad in a baggy gray suit and Hush Puppies,
showed up weekly rolling his cart of tone-bells and crusty
    music
books up and down the aisles
rapping us on the head with a mallet if we weren't singing
"Drill Ye Tarriers" properly.

Ms. Kaner flung fresh dittos at us
that we sniffed with glee before she led us
in "Brand New Key,"
a tune by some hippie named Melanie.

"I've been looking around a while,
you've got something for me …"
we warbled before chords struck
on all of us and we landed
on Planet Music.

Fish Out of Water

I'd never heard of the Whiffenpoofs,
who, glowing in white gloves and tails,
sing a cappella in the corner near the fire
      while I stand, broken
toothpick in hand,
wondering how it's all done –
the caviar hidden in my crumpled napkin –
cradling my wineglass
acting like I belong.

The ladies of the Junior League
adorned in Bergdorf dresses,
kiss the air in their made-up faces
size each other up,
clink their glasses,
jiggle ice,
hope for a slot at the yacht club.

      Only the qualified will be admitted.

From Minnesota, I have landed on Planet Greenwich
where Captains of Wall Street
prance around each other
in Gucci loafers (no socks), slicked back hair
gold-buttoned blazers –
the final arbiters of the chosen sailors.

Back home in his garage
Harvey, clad in flannel,
fires up his frying pan,

lowers the walleye he caught
on his outboard last weekend
into sizzling oil
while the neighborhood folks
appear with their beer
listening for the whippoorwills,

no credentials needed.

Before

In the movie about my street
our parents are still alive
and we children don't yet know
about their drinking,
their touching,
their brushes with infidelity,
their looming heart failures and cancers
barreling toward the funeral home on the corner
where we'll one day gather
to make small talk –
reminisce about the fish fries
on the 4th of July.

In my movie, we're back
barefoot in our fresh pajamas
waiting for the Mister Softee truck to make its rounds.
We still love the feeling
of cool evening grass
as we twirl our sparklers, tickle the air
with blazing diamonds that jump and swirl
before they disappear,
before the first house burns down
before the father next door
gets locked up for
his unholy actions,
or
before the boy from the saddest family
puts a pistol to his head

leaving us

waving shriveling, smoldering
gray wands,
their glowing specks of light preserved only
on brittle reels of film
now piled next to a broken projector,
in someone's attic, no replacement parts available.

Breaking

Between the shelf and the floor

the fragile glass floated in air.

I knew it would crash –
yet how beautiful,
how crystal clear
for that fleeting moment
it was
when I reached for it,
but missed.

Down the Rabbit Hole

When I Googled Keebler Elves
I was immediately sent to a 1853
bakery plopped down in
Philadelphia, the sixth most populated city in the United
    States.

Abruptly I landed in the commonwealth of Kentucky,
found myself wading along the banks
of the Ohio River, then on to Lake Erie
where – without warning –
discovered my feet sinking into Sub-Saharan Africa
which led me to the Iron age, preceded by the Stone Age.

Surprise! Herodotus entered,
stage left
back to the Roman Conquest and the Viking Age,
where I clicked and linked
until I was floating near
the Faroe Islands,
halfway between Norway and Scotland.

The sub polar oceanic climate—
windy, wet, cloudy, cool—was too much.

It was lunch time
so I logged out,
shut down,
and returned to my sofa—
Keebler, my long-haired tabby,
snuggled into my side, a fur ball of charm
curled up in his own jungle of dreams.

Driven

Bogie, the lumpy mascot of the football team
whose brazen audacity
outshone his bad acne,
made us roar with laughter,
always the entertainer.

Those of us who dared hop into his junky red Ford
— the one with bald tires —
bragged that we'd survived
one of his wild rides as he wove
in and out of traffic doing his 3 Stooges imitations
spinning the wheel as though he were immortal,
dodging semi-trucks and avoiding head-on collisions by a
    hair.

Oh how brave we all were
until a decade later at the silent funeral where
tales of the past stopped dead in their tracks,
Bogie's totaled car now scraps
for someone else's repairs.

Game Over

The quarterback, dressed
in school colors (red and white),
lies in his coffin,
face caked in foundation,
as the pastor rambles on
promising us our star
has reached the end zone,
executed his final touchdown:
Jesus the ultimate goal post.

Those of us still left in the stands
marvel at the years now vanished
since those Friday night games, decades ago.

Our hair gone gray or plain just gone —
we're not cheering, not clapping.
No confetti,
no marching band,
no concession stand,
just ham sandwiches, coffee,
cookies and punch,
the bunch of us confessing
old crushes, imagining
alternative game changers
before life intercepted those passes.

Gospel Billboards

WHERE ARE YOU GOING?
HEAVEN OR HELL?
Dial 855-FOR TRUTH

I pull over, dial for answers.
These operators must know:
The Lord told them so!

Regarding eternal salvation,
  — all I need —
to do is to press #2,
and then press #3, hope that Jesus will save me.

Red lights flash
in my rear-view mirror:

Expired registration?
No Visa application?
Here it comes: the sanctimonious proclamation.

I zip up my flame
retardant vest.

I'm ready.

Sound Field

Silent as the hollow
Mailbox outside
Today no news
Just an echoing
Nothingness from somewhere in space
Drifts across the prairies
Of my thoughts
Wind combing wheat
Quiet from where I sit
But loud as the combine that threshes
Grasshoppers crackle, snap,
Jump, escape the harvester's teeth

Silent now fallow field
Husks wide open to blistering sun

Small Print

It was always there
the small print
word after word sentence
after sentence paragraph
after paragraph page
after page
too voluminous to absorb
too small to bother with
until one day
it really mattered and there was no recourse
just alphabet soup
boiling letters into disintegration
e's becoming i's or l's
that were once's p's or q's?
The blur indecipherable
The regret indescribable

Passing

Into this world I passed through the birth canal.

The doctor passed me to the nurse who passed me to my mother.

Once home, the grandmas passed me around as I passed gas

then learned how to pass the milk, the potatoes and the time away.

Later, I passed kindergarten, then all twelve grades, college and graduate school.

I began to pass blood when I was 13 while older girls passed along their advice as I passed into my womanhood, strolling through the tampon aisle for 34 more years.

I got passed up for positions: crossing guard, 1st place in anything, a job at McDonald's, the cheerleading squad, the school plays. I failed my 1st driver's test, but thank God, passed the second time, learned how to pass others safely but preferred to stay behind the slowpokes because it was safer. In high school, joints and booze were passed around, and I only passed out once as I passed through those rites of passage. Men didn't make passes at lasses with glasses, so I graduated to contacts and pretty soon I was passing for pretty and the phone began ringing. My grandpa passed away when I was 17, and once that was past, I passed my high school exams, all the while passing daily notes to my best friend in the hallways between classes. Soon I was in college passing new boys on the sidewalk who passed in and out of my life. Always, I was trying to pass for 19, the drinking age at the time. I didn't want life to pass me by, so I passed on a job in Minnesota and flew to New York, passing into my next phase, which started as a nanny at the yacht club watching all those preppies pass by the pool wearing pearl earrings – talking not of Michelangelo but of Bloomingdales and Lord and Taylor and wallpaper samples. I didn't aspire to this, so I passed up the chance to become a Wall Street

Banker's housewife. For a while, I didn't pass up the chance to be an idiot and make a fool of myself over and over in backseats of cars in Connecticut country club parking lots. Could a girl from Coon Rapids, Minnesota, pass for a Yale graduate? Sometimes.

I finally fell in love and passed through the neighborhoods of Manhattan, gobbling up dinners and cocktails at 5-star restaurants, South Street Seaport, passing the weekends at the Met, in the Village, Soho, Chelsea. The time passed so quickly and soon the proposal came. It was time to become an adult. I couldn't pass it up. I passed muster with the in-laws, the required courses without reading "Remembrance of Things Past," (passing over poor old Proust) and became a certified professional educator. I wrote hall passes, passed students when they succeeded, passed my weekends grading papers, until one day, my husband suddenly passed away, and all my joy got stuck in the past, at least for a while. But once time passed, the sun came out and I passed Go, collecting more than $200. I got past it, at least for now, and someday strangers will wander past my grave without giving me a passing thought.

Seat Assignments

"On the right side,
you'll see Mount Everest,"
announces the voice from the cockpit
35,000 feet
above sea level.

But I'm on the left side,
the other side, the wrong side,
stuck in the middle –
nothing but clouds out my window,
nothing but the heads across the aisle
blocking the summit
as they lean toward the light,
gaze at the highest peak on the globe,
their oohs and aahs drifting through the cabin.

The seat in front of me is all I see:
a plastic cup on a flimsy tray table,
a stomach distress bag,
the in-flight magazine, its dog-eared pages
illustrating flight routes to places I'll never go.

On the same plane
we'll reach our destination,
touch down
in the same place,
exiting with different views:
those who saw,
those who didn't.

No Show

Perhaps after six years of missing
all of those concerts, he'd finally see
her in the center on the highest riser
(careful not to fall back)
belting out Joy to the World
or mournfully bleating like
the little lamb to the shepherd boy:

"Do you see what I see?
A child, a child shivers in the cold ..."

Perhaps he'd finally hear
her song high above the sea
washing over the rest of the parents
beaming in their folding chairs
as they listened to their children sing
O Come All Ye Faithful
before they filed out
of the gymnasium
back into the cold
Silent Night.

Situation Comedy

At 104 she
still smears
her lipstick
around her mouth
tiny chunks of red
crumbling off her face
as she lurches toward the dining room
clinging to her walker
clutching the brakes
for another meal of meat
loaf, mashed
potatoes, and Jello with her table mates
Grace and Lloyd
whom she secretly calls Grease and Lard.

Something has to be funny about all of this.

D. E. Green

D. E. Green taught English at Augsburg University for 33 years and has published articles on Shakespeare, general-interest essays, and poetry. His poem "Gratitude" won the 2018 *Martin Lake Journal* Bookend Prize; other work has appeared in "Bright Light Stories in the Night" (Southeastern Minnesota Poets, 2021, 2022); in the Red Wing Arts' Poet-Artist Collaboration (2021, 2022); in *Third Wednesday*; in *Lost Lake Folk Opera*; in *Willows Wept Review*; in "Visual Verse: An Anthology of Art and Words," with Peter Sorel's photographs in "Lake/Sky" (2014); and on the sidewalks of his hometown, Northfield, Minnesota. Three of his poems were recognized in the 2022 League of Minnesota Poets Contest. His collection, "Jumping the Median," was published in 2019; his chapbook, "Catastrophizing in Catastrophe" in 2023. Previously published poems in "We Look West" include "Dragonfly Love" in *Willows Wept Review* and the 2021 Red Wing Arts' Poet-Artist Collaboration, "Because Love" in *Lost Lake Folk Opera*, "You can't imagine" in *Visual Verse*, "Hang Your Head" in *Visual Verse* and "Catastrophizing in Catastrophe, Unexpected Gift" in *Lost Lake Folk Opera*, and "Against Metaphor" in *Willows Wept Review*. Jointly, with spouse Becky Boling, Green serves as Interim Northfield Poet Laureate.

Dragonfly Love

Most mornings I wake to rise
and fall of breath, yours and mine,
syncopated chuff and hush
of animating spirits. Between us,
as material as the son I'd bring you
to suckle in the night, invisible
threads stretch, like airy webs
blue needles, darting over marsh,
weave amid the swaying cattails.

For Becky: Love Sonnet after Neruda

I don't love you as if there were no morrow,
as if I could imagine a dawn waking
without you. I love you unthinkingly
like a deep breath, a careless yawn, a sigh.

I love you like the mortified mother-
in-law's tongue in our living room you water
when the spirit moves you, like the dust blanketing
so delicately your beloved whatnots.

I love you like our motions every morn,
like the last cup of overheated coffee—
without regard to taste or over-
doing it. I love you like this because
I know no other way, simply cannot
go on without your necessary presence.

Whistle Down the Wind

here is the crinkling cold
purple lips pressed
tulip to tulip
lost loves lost hearts
the old kisses like the newer
gone to seed gone to sea
whistled down the wind
an old ballad soughing
on night breezes cold
starry sky sparkling
black with scattered diamonds

and then the question
always the question
returns to haunt this chill beauty
this enchanting desolation

Why? it whispers *Why?*

and the interrogative night
the pervasive dark whispers
whistles wails that *why?*
which contains the eye of the I
but remains unanswered
unanswerable like a child's grave
like the lightning strike the tsunami
the tornado the rending quake
our anthill devastation
desperate antennae flailing
heart loss love loss lament

the electric need for contact
for spark even as the world is dying

and this is our song now
a syncopated eclipse
melodic murmuration
unending ululation
at nature's graveside
but also a last lyrical joy
a dance macabre but festive
a mardi gras of loss and love
bodies turning and turning
toward each other and away
until the spirit quiets
until the soul hears its own breath

inhale exhale inhale exhale inhale
hear the inspiration
hear the expiration
our souls' breath a breeze
across the frozen plains of earth and hearts
across the land animate and inanimate
across the waste we've made
our own undoing

let us sing now here at the end
clasp hands
feel neighbor knuckles against our palms

let loose a dirge more beautiful than life
to welcome death
and wash our sorrows from this world

Local Report

The weather was inside:
Chill and bone dry.
Dark as a moonless sky.

The weather was inside.
Wind howled across the bay.
It whirled my heart away.

The weather was inside.
It rained my grief
and yours—brown leaf.

The weather was inside.
And that is where I'll keep it.
That is where I'll hide.

Just Dog & Man

Sometimes it should be like that.
Lonesome. Just dog & man.
No other people—or dogs—to distract
us from each other and our concentration
on this cold and lonely autumn world.
Some of the trees still pop their red,
gold, orange leaf bursts
even though the sky is leaden
just hints of blue and light
in the East. I remember my dawn,
rising each new day, imagining
it would all be different today—
or could be. Better. I always wanted
better but ended up with good enough.
Which is enough. Most folks don't
even get that: Enough. Though we
have all had enough—of the way
things are. Of that kind of enough
we've had plenty. So I'm okay
today with our being just dog & man.
A perfect couple. Silent but purposeful,
on this quiet overcast morning
moving block by block by block toward
a future that will have to be enough.

Because Love

We cannot

go out and have fun
dine, without planning, at Reunion
attend theater—at all

make a move without risk assessment
celebrate birthdays *en masse*
luxuriate in hugging our friends

escape these four walls
avoid the feeling of entrapment
sing our joys when Joy itself has fled

We cannot

find a light at the end of this mine shaft
rise to the surface of these deep woes
hope for a future better than our past

see democracy thriving
hear ourselves, the people, calling to each other
shake the unworthy from the seats of power

We must not

stifle our generosity
stymy our will to act
flag in our determination to be and do better

Even if
everything seems lost
Even if
we can't imagine the dawn we once believed in
Even if
compassion and love have been confined to our solitary
   hearts

We can, despite winter, still

come to the town square
shout from our doorsteps and windows
resist the howls of the haters

Because
love in the face of such hatred is the only way
Because
without love, buried so deeply within us, we cannot survive
Because
we need each other, my loves, at this dark moment in this
   dark place.

Giving Up

He can swim
a long time
back and forth
in the Olympic pool.
Out far beyond
the sand bar
in the big lake.
Beyond the breakers
in the rolling ocean.

Sometimes he empties
his lungs of every breath
feels the body's weight
in water and the sinking
start. He would like
to let go. He would like
to move down into this
watery cool world—
surrender everything.

But he doesn't.
He can't.
Not out of fear.
Just the impulse
for love and air.

Feeding the Lions

Each morning, after my own ablutions,
I put on my uniform, the bright blue,
fill the green pail with bloody red meat,
and go out to feed the lions.

My lions.

I'm not sure how I collected them.
But there they are, my private menagerie,
demanding that I feed them, pay them attention,
even fear them.

I don't.

But they do wear me out and down—
not so much in tossing hunks of flesh
in their direction as in the ceaselessness
of the chore. They're always hungry.

What I wouldn't give for one day off?

They roar their need,
demand I return
with more slaughtered flesh.
It might as well be my own.

They are roaring still.

You can't imagine

what it was like before
plastic. The sun shone
softly over fields. Earth
buried the dead as they fell.

We didn't carry extinction
in eternal shopping bags.
We didn't swelter beneath
our once lifegiving star.

The ghosts of ancestors
rested beside us, protected
us. Now the searing heat
has dried those souls.

We poisoned the waters.
The dust of the past
balloons as we shuffle
across our dead planet.

Hang Your Head

As I hang mine.
We are forlorn
horses in a barren
field, heads drooping
over brown stubble.

We have sad, dark
eyes. Rivers of sweat
run down our flanks,
streaking our blue-black
hides with rust-red
dampened dust.

We seem, to passing
eyes, the saddest
creatures—without
sustenance, without
purpose. And yet.

Here we are, nibbling
still at the yellow
tufts of nothing
before us. Making
do. Surviving. Till,
again, we thrive.

Unexpected Gift
for Tom

We didn't expect you—
a late arrival. After we thought
we knew the us that we were.
You altered our calculus—
Cathy and I changed diapers
while Mom went out to work
and Dad adjusted to the fact
of you. You two hit it off.
Bigtime. You were and are
the most like him. The rest
of us couldn't give a damn
about football or baseball.
We shared movies with Dad,
but you've shared all his passions—
he even coached your Little League team!—
and his affability, gregariousness,
and charm. So we need you,
baby brother, our littlest and last,
our very best. You can't check out
before the rest of us leave the room.
Your mirth and wit, always tinged
with love. Your letters—so like Dad's
own weepies—full of gratitude
for Beth and the kids, Dad and Mom,
and sometimes even us sibs. We
need you at this dark time, in this
dark year, to lighten our lives.

The End

They keep wanting
stuff from me
all these people
around me and then
they act aggravated
if I look exasperated
am exasperated
because I'm retired
now supposedly
and I shouldn't
have to do anything
I don't want to do
and I'm perfectly
fine foraging for food
in the fridge or the co-op
or Econo Foods (which
is something else
now, I forget the name)
and I just want to
do what I want to
do which is mostly
nothing just read
and write and sometimes
walk the dog but
only when I want to
and I want to eat
cheese again whenever
I want it and pizza
and grapefruit
after all I only

have a decade
or maybe two
to do whatever
it is I retired
to do which frankly
escapes me like
so much these days
which grow shorter
in winter and seem
to stay short even
in summer and
they're going fast
so fast even though
dinner never comes
fast enough and
every day someone
has something they
want from me and
I suppose that's nice
to be wanted and I do
sometimes like to do
what I'm asked because
the other person smiles
someone I used to know
well and it just seems
the right thing to do
(doesn't it?) to spend
my last days making all
these people happy.

Nesting: Morelia, Mexico
February 2023

We're back after the strictures of pandemic
have relaxed and we can negotiate moving
through airports and enclosed cabins in flight.

We're here. Ferreting away our few necessities.
Making of our friends' spare room a temporary
roost, a comfy nest for our short southern sojourn
in midwinter. We always build a home away

from home. It's just our way. We look around
and figure out where this and that go, arrangements
that produce just what we need: an illusion
we belong here, have always been, will always
be—despite the truth we know—right here.

Nesting is what we do. It keeps at bay
the fearsome fact: there is no place to stay.

Another Poet's Car

I like driving someone else's vehicle
checking out all the bells and whistles
it offers me—or lack thereof.

I like trying it out, seeing if
the ride is smoother than my own
toying with the idea of stealing it
imagining that really all the cars
belong to all of us so this one is mine too.

Even though it's not, I'm going to keep
driving it a little farther down the road—
thankful for the ride—
until a better one comes along.

Long Marriage

In the morning after exercises
I release the dog from his kennel.
We descend the stairs, disturb
you writing in your journal.
There's a cup of lukewarm
coffee with soy on the counter.
I chug it, with my pills (to stave
off death), and head out
into the snow with the dog.
We trudge for about three-quarters
of an hour in the bitter landscape.
When I return, there it is again,
that lukewarm cup of coffee with soy.

Against Metaphor

Moss is moss and not another thing.
Woodpeckers, woodpeckers, and not
words on the wing. Old robin's
robin—neighborly plain
bird flitting here and
there. Cardinals,
red—simple
striking
sight.

Steve McCown

Pushcart nominee **Steve McCown** has published poems in *Lost Lake Folk Opera Magazine, Willows Wept Review, Colorado Crossing, Arizona Western Voice, Bright Lights Stories in the Night,* Minnesota Public Radio's *End in Mind project,* the 2023 *Red Wing Poet-Artist Collaboration,* as well as in *Legacies: Poetic Living Wills, Minnesota Writes, Minnesota Reads e-library.* His poem "The Bridge at Bridge Square" was included in *Northfield Poetry Tours: Poems about Northfield Places.* In 2020, Shipwreckt Books Publishing Company of Winona, Minnesota, released McCown's poetry collection, "Ghosting." After teaching high school and college English on the deserts of California and Arizona for over 30 years, McCown now lives in beautiful Northfield, Minnesota, where five of his poems are stamped in the sidewalks.

Automatons

Power on,
the chain-link conveyor belt
bolted to the ceiling
creaks, groans, rumbles,
signaling another day of work.

Dangling from hooks,
wooden chair parts
(arms, legs, backs)
turn and sway,
jiggle past us—

an endless mobile
endlessly configuring
a confined space.

We prep surfaces,
sand oak, maple,
enhance dark
grainy patterns,
the swirling mysteries
missing from our lives
brought to life.

Rubbed ragged,
the grit scratches
away fingerprints,
and the transcendent dust
clouds eyes, clogs throats.

Through the haze
we can hardly see,
but the parts move along
(soon assembled)
and the punch clock ticks.

Balancing Act

At this windy height,
everything aslant,
sky, roof, ladder, me.

Scrub-pine needles
sticking out like fish bones
clog gutters, a wasp nest
chokes a drainpipe.

Bugs, feathers, eggshells
compacted, mud caked.
Rain stopped in its tracks,
nothing washed away,
purged.

Wobbling on a rung,
I slop debris,
the dead, over and out,
onto dry grass,
create a scant flow,
liberate a trickle.

Clear of gutters,
yet within reach,
a maple streams bronze and gold.

Hands grubbing in muck,
my eyes land on leaves—
I could easily fall into them,
fall for them, be swept away.

Night Basketball

Under a cloudy moon
I could barely
see the rim,
but making the shot
didn't matter.

The ball rattled
metal backboards,
shook chain-link nets
like rough chimes.

Each sound—
swishing, bouncing, ricocheting—
declared my presence
on the empty playground

and bore its message
across the street
to her open window,
calling her out.

Together in darkness
we played
one-on-one
beneath jangling nets.

Contents of a Cedar Chest

It isn't the soft Canadian wool blankets
scattered with moth balls
like toxic hailstones,

or the summer sheets
absorbing acrid fumes
like bad dreams,

or the surviving moths
attacking Father's decorated Army uniform
folded at the bottom.

It's the chest itself.
When empty, it isn't.

Bands of crimson and orange
and russet rise
or set every time I open
and close the lid—an ingrained sun.

Free of fumes,
a rich redolence emerges,
a treasure trove of earthy scents
deeply inhaled,
transporting me far away—

into the North Woods,
into the heart of cedar.

Coloring in a Care Center

for Virginia *Ruttan*, 1930-2023

Stark white,
like snow suspended,
the pages face her.

Black outlines
the bare bones
of people, houses, trees, birds.

Interiors empty,
nothing filled in.

To the art at hand,
she brings boxed crayons,
a grit eraser,
a sealed packet of bright pencils,
all her senses.

She stays within the lines,
but the colors emerge,
transcend confinement.

A caged fan stands out,
blades petal-like,
multi-hued—they whirl
flamboyantly.

You feel the breath of green,
indigo and crimson,
of orange, amber, and yellow
radiate across her room.

Deconstruction

Halloween displaced—
our cemetery won't stay put.

A gust dislodges a Gothic tombstone,
the skull-emblazoned RIP
careening across the street,
end clunking end over end.

White sheets billowing
on bare branches spirit away.

Caught in an updraft,
a gigantic cobweb snaps,
rises, catches something
somewhere.

A glass-eyed tarantula,
suddenly animated,
scurries off.

Recalcitrant, unstable,
our props and symbols elude us,
the grounds keepers—

levitating over heads,
beyond our grasp,
a black veiled witch's hat.

Touring My Ghost Town

In this parking lot
a brownstone U.S. Post Office
with Corinthian columns
and marble steps stood
before urban renewal
moved in and sent everything packing.

Here, in an empty alley,
a door opened to Buck's Novelties,
a Ma and Pa store,
gag toys aplenty—chattering teeth,
hand buzzers, canned rubber snakes.

A lone pinball machine lit up the shop,
popcorn always popping,
glass jars crammed with rock candy.

On that block
crowded with duplexes,
a statue of a feathered Indian Princess
topped a Victorian fountain,
hand over an eye as if she
were seeing something in the distance.

Cast iron pelicans and turtles
circled her solitary prominence,
spewed water, greened
over time in the sunlight,
in the rain.

Over there, a billiards hall,
The Hurry Back,
where we played snooker,
smoked Swisher Sweets,
acted twice our age,
is nothing now
to hurry back to.

And here am I,
alone–relic and revenant.

Homemade

I've been turning it over ever since,
how grandfather made heaven
from rock salt, ice, sugar, cream

as he stood in the dark at the bottom
of basement steps
late at night (coal bin behind him).

He cranked an iron lever
on a small wood box around
and around and around,

muscled the ingredients together,
adjusted other levers,
manipulated heat and cold.

Then stopped. He opened
the lid—and my eyes' taste buds—
to ice cream, a brightness

shining up to me
at the top of the stairs,
a pure sweetness too soon devoured,

savored for years,
as if I had eaten
a lasting source of light.

In an Antique Store

1.
Pushed to the back of a shelf,
behind plastic flowers,
a chipped statue
of Jackie Robinson
(playing days long gone).

I ease it out into the light.

2.
A silent aisle.
No ticking here, no pulse.

Unwound, unplugged,
wood clocks keep stopped time.

Hands frozen on various numbers
mark hours as if —then
and still—special.

3.
A few rows over,
orange Fiesta plates the same as Mother's.
Carnival glass, crystal goblets,
and a midnight blue vase recall Grandmother.

Jugs, stools, a child's chair, a toy horse,
all decorated with faded rosemaling,
like Mother's and Grandmother's,
crowd a back room.

Too many, too much
to take in at once—
dusty excess of nostalgia.

4.
Here's a Lionel train set like mine,
going nowhere in an old box.

A red Tonka truck, well-traveled,
is missing a wheel.

A miniature Tom Thumb cash register
still rings up cent signs
in a cloudy window.

5.
I drift from aisle to aisle.
These items date me,
will survive me.

I wonder if the train still runs.

Percussion

for Ken B.

In our old town,
alone,
he loves hard surfaces,
the accompaniment of concrete.

A wing tip tap dancer
dancing with echoes,
he sparks notes
from a cracked sidewalk, a dark street.

Lightly, he renders
a vacant parking lot melodious.
Asphalt softens,
resonant under the touch of his shoes.

The clicking toe-and-heel metal
on worn soles,
over a scruffy brick alley,
evokes the music within,
pure substance of sound

breaking through our shells,
breaking them apart.

Sleight of Hand
for my grandmother

Arthritis gnarls, knots her fingers.

Still, she dips into blue
a fine-tipped brush,
dabs image after image

on canvass— prairie wind,
big sky and a creek wandering
through a field of chicory.

Taking up a needle,
she stitches abalone buttons
on a cowgirl shirt,

a vest, fastens
silver conchos around
a leather belt.

She scissors dandelions,
ferments wine
to yellow-amber.

Performs sleights
with ranch eggs,
two at once,

one handed,
tap, tapping them against
a mixing bowl rim,

yolk after yolk
after yolk
freed from hard shells

slide whole,
intact,
to the bottom—

awhirl with a dozen suns.

Writing Materials

Corn cobs
salvaged from an old granary
were spiny quills
dipped into a tin of kerosine,
clear ink.

Tips down,
drop by inflammable drop
we drizzled our names,
lit them with wooden matchsticks.

Ignited, the letters flared,
illuminated a bare patch
behind a weathered barn—

our names dancing
on hard ground,
rising like firebirds
from a sheet of dirt.

Genesis

From caterpillar
to chrysalis to dread—
my neighbor on vacation
put me in charge
of what will become.

Two have already become,
flexing wings,
blood flowing through
a filigree of veins.

Trembling,
I unzip suspended
delicate mesh netting
like a veiled womb,
squeeze a sugar solution
from a syringe onto
a circular red sponge.

Shadowing
this swaying world,
my hand grazes
a green chrysalis,
nudges another pupa,
brushes an orange-black,
white-spotted wing
breaking free.

An intruder,
I fumble in genesis.
A quivering monarch
clings to a stick.

Acolyte

Eyes on the altar,
back to the congregation,
I lit thin candles,
then withdrew to the wings.

Sermon ended. Amen.
Somber organ beckoning me,
I snuffed the flames.
White wisps vanished, spirited away.

Now I hang prisms in windows,
fill feeders with sunflower
seeds, wait, watch
for a blazing cardinal to alight,
or a visitation of songbirds.

A Pinging in the Dark

1.
We bring her into our house,
center her on the dining room table,
amidst yellow day lilies and candles.

For weeks she will stay there,
a poster picture of a missing girl.

Only her freckled face shows,
a closeup (the rest cropped out)
against a grainy blue background.
She is smiling.

Listed in the margin, on the edge:
fifteen, 5 feet 7,
red brown hair,
wears glasses,
without her medication.

She is white and black.
Her parents—beside themselves
on the front porch,
missing as well, mother
facing a blank slate— said a pinging,
a single sharp note,
led them to our town.

Pray to hear a voice
in the all-night lit up darkness
of their home miles away.

2.
She is everywhere—
pinned to a public bulletin board,

taped on a sliding glass door at Family Fare,
displayed in a youth center,
and tacked to a weathered telephone pole,
a splintery crack running from top
to bottom, wide behind the picture.

I've seen her, you have too,
we all have, again
and again …

In Memory

for J.A.

He kept the dead in a metal box engraved with dates—
pictures once presented as human evidence in Nuremberg,
where he stood at an inner courtroom door—an honorary
    guard.

G. I. rations, canteen, in hand, M1 rifle slung over
a shoulder, heavy camera strapped around
his neck, he had trudged under a lettered iron arch:

ARBEIT MACHT FREI

The photographs rested on a marble mantel above a brick
    fireplace,
flickered year-round in a dark chamber of his memory.
He would never burn them.

Julie A. Ryan

Julie A. Ryan is a poet, essayist, novelist, and visual artist. Her poems, essays, and prose have appeared in a variety of publications. "Candy Cigarettes" and "We Look West" appeared in *Relative Space*. "Plowed Under" appeared in *Willows Wept Review*. "Another Chance Also Rises" appeared in *Relative Space*. Her poems and essays have also appeared in *End in Mind Pandemic Poetry Project, Northfield Sidewalk Poetry, Visual Verse: an Anthology of Art and Words, Lost Lake Folk Opera, The Clothesline Review,* and Minnesota newspapers. Her collection of concrete poems, "Relative Space," was published in 2021, and her socially relevant fictional trilogy, "When Life Was Still," was released in 2020. Since childhood, she has been interested in nature, wordplay, design, math, science, and humanitarian issues—themes that frequently coexist in her writing projects today.

Goodnight, Sweet Dreams

Sometimes wind is just wind.

This spring's breezy
plum tree blossoms
produced dreams of possibility

that plopped unpredictably
from twisters
hopping through summer

and precipitated fermentation
under pulpy swirls
of autumnal regret . . .

only to be swept
into the murky blizzard
of winter's terminal grip.

Sometimes wind is an omen.

Candy Cigarettes

We saved our candy cigarettes for cold weather,
smoking Lucky Lights
to blow thoughtless clouds at each other—
just like the grown-ups
we wanted to become—
while waiting for the school bus

that would deliver us
to either bullies and crabby teachers
or extra recess and chocolate milk breaks.
That patch of gravel with ruts to the left and the right
wrapped in crisp sky outlined with sunrise
was the one world we ruled.

Just us, and whoever we wanted to be,
calling the shots, the top of our lungs
joining the fun between puffs with jingles
about Oscar Mayer, Coke, McDonald's, Band-Aids,
ballads about bows and flows of angel hair, country roads,
tin soldiers, and begging Billy not to be a hero.

Imagined nicotine, sugar, and endorphins
laced our brains
and we did our happy-go-lucky dance,
blissfully lost in the momentary air we controlled,
completely addicted
to candy cigarettes and singing.

Parchment

My words have run dry.

Inklings once somersaulting
from my joyful pen
and lingual stunts flowing from my tongue
are now blotted, tied up,
locked behind the prison
of your victorious finger
held to my lips
in a chronic "shush."

But Dali's dripping clock
ticks in my tock
and says it's time
to be loyal to my colorful truth,
cut loose with paint
in languages you can't grasp—
a cathartic, roaring golden-blue rain
of acrylic and oil

to whet this arid voice.

The Invitation

Tell me when the mourning should begin—
yesterday, when I received the invitation
to your going-away party;
tomorrow, when we'll embrace
your best qualities one last time,
or when your adventure finally ends?

Right now, it's morning in Hawaii,
my mind sails as life's fleeting nature catches up with me—
dives into rainbows of waterfalls.
Fantastical flora and fauna offer escape;
meditation on fish weaving through crystal blue waves
leads to lush islands made for disappearing

from the situation etched in your invitation.
I won't know the right words to say at your gathering
where you'll concentrate your eyes on loved ones,
creating a pillow of memories to rest your chemo brain.
I don't want to encourage your departure
from your new rocky terrain,

so when I show up at your so-called celebration,
I guess I'll just say Aloha
and hope that you'll focus on love,
fellowship,
the hello side of life,
not the good-bye.

It Bites

I let go
and the dust of what
our relationship could have been
finally sits
at the back of my teeth
to be revisited again and again
with a sweep
of my regretful tongue
while Freddy Mercury's vinyl screams
taunt me—
         another one
         another one
         another one
of my intimate defeats.

Olive Branches

Inspired by the Immersive Van Gogh Exhibit

Can we hold these colorful heart-gripping notes forever—
the ones written by Handel,
Thom Yorke,
and Imogen Heap?

Together, they speak to our creative souls
like whispers in Van Gogh's frosted *Starry Night* from our
    better days,
like the hum in his syncopated *Sunflowers*
that dance around our disrupted rhythm.

While sitting cross-legged—side by side on the floor—
we focus our eyes on the same page as we study the
    movement
of monumental *Irises*
transcending twists defining their existence.

From the corner of my idealized scenes finger-painted
with drips of fairy tales we once wrote,
chords of harmony sweep
away the toxic lead of our past

and strokes of vibrant yellow blend
into the edges of your raw sienna silhouette.

Diminished Interlude

for Grandma
Inspired by strokes, jazz, rights, wrongs,
and Barack Obama

It's the notes you didn't play
that sing in my recollection.
You didn't have time to listen
to Miles Davis and Coltrane, to read Baldwin.

Did the stuttering spin of your distorted mind
find that the hammering of neural pathways
harmonized with the stammering
of your ums—

the ums that were the utterance
of everything our relationship had become?
The gaps between guttural sounds
shouted through the pounding of flat keys

about all the unfinished runs—
milestones unachieved,
moments unspent
making memories.

After you passed, the spaces hardened
with the onomatopoeia
of silent cement—a weight that casts
a warning of my own sounds to come.

It's the stop of your swing
and your blues,

the shadow of your steps
not taken that have haunted me ever since
your bebop
improvisation
        was
            done.

'68 Comeback Special

An antiseptic percussion of blues in the background,
I stood in the newly found light
of a rock 'n' roll tunnel,
or maybe I was just propped up
under a halogen operating room lamp
hanging over my amplified heart
that suddenly stopped.

I waited for Elvis to greet me with open arms
and those fun hips that offended Ed Sullivan's audience—
the hips that fit in the *'68 Comeback Special* pants
from the same year I was born
and made Elvis look so good that I decided,
when I saw the rerun of the special at the age of four,
I probably should marry Elvis someday.

I waited
and waited
and waited,
waited in that sterile flatline glow
for twenty-three minutes
with an eager smile on my dead face,
sure the ghost of Elvis would show.

Then my tender heart was tha-wumped,
by defibrillator paddles
and the hollow understanding
that I was stood up
by Elvis
in the special pants.

Plowed Under

Songs I sang in the field when I was a child re-emerge
as I now dread being mowed down too soon,
dead in my tracks,
while knee-deep in muddled dreams.

I want to take John Denver's country roads home
once more, see the sun come up,
rake these fading farm-girl fingers
through wild plans and rows of tangled knots

to unearth the messy plot that buried ambitions,
kept me from reaching the end
of trails where I might find success
and the place I belong.

At the OK Corral

If I open my new heart to you, will you corral it,
cage it in stainless steel wires,
lock it behind bars of the Bee Gees' "Stayin' Alive,"
or frame it in bleeding red drips of Jim Dine's paint?

Thoughts tumbleweed across
the ghost town of my post-op mind,
politely mumbling
that everything is OK, fine as always.

If my blipping pulse continues to buck
when faced with curiosity about my well-being on this
     cardiac desert,
will you politely run with my refurbished hum,
weathered hands outstretched, accepting any texture of
     normalcy?

Or will my mechanical ways drive you crazy,
make you reach for holsters of fluttering memories
from when my heart was real, pulsating perfectly
in the palm of how you thought our adventure would be?

Don't Stop Thinking About Tomorrow

Despite Fleetwood Mac's command
blasting over and over on the radio,
I *do* look back,
through a haunted windowpane.

In the dead of my desire
for the fiery dawn
of better days,
the waning moon hangs burnt red.

Powder Remains After a Fire

*Excerpts from "How to Speak Poetry" by Leonard Cohen

Leonard Cohen was right:
Poetry is life.
Poetry is ash.
Nothing more, nothing less.

Not a contest.
Not a symbol of status.
Not a stratosphere reserved
for the elite.

The best poems flow from unfiltered poets,
polluted with truth,
whose absolute words bleed in audiences' ears
when cutting to the meat of their unwrapped journeys,

from renegade poets, who don't try on stage
"to impersonate a butterfly,"* bunny hug their muse,
or radiate drama
with attempts to "invent a sunny day,"*

from satiated poets who don't "hunger for applause"*
but cause the masses to sit up and hear
by chewing on lines
from the tangled side of reality,

from lowly poets without "noble intentions,"*
who rise above, with true grit,
by resisting
manicured walls of restrictions,

from liberated poets who dive in,
rolling in juicy scraps on editing-room floors

to wrestle with stanzas
that threaten the poetically timid,

from plainspoken poets who "avoid the flourish,"*
preferring to accent accuracy
when examining spawn
from the nakedness of existence,

from driven poets who are unchained, untethered
to literary guidelines
while free-versing
new paths through the rhythmic world,

from hurling poets who bypass conformity,
ever-evolving
while tumbling heart-first
through sharp critiques,

from raw poets who never stop to mourn
misunderstandings
or patch perpetual wounds
inflicted by the poetry police.

Life's best poets are cracked—without pretentious skin,
open fleshed—who gladly forget the "perfect offering"
that Leonard Cohen rejects
as his "Anthem" sings, "That's how the light gets in."

Another Chance Also Rises

I want another chance
to dance with the descendants
of Hemingway's six-toed cats.

I wasted that trip to Key West obsessing
about crawling into the typewriter
displayed on Papa's desk

so that I might drown
in his ink and give my existence
some meaning.

Before I got to the Southernmost Point,
I think I stared too long into the mouth
of that roadside alligator

and saw that my life was dangling
like the debris
strung across his teeth.

The only remedy I could see
was escaping to the sunken resting place
carved by the Father of Icebergs.

I let myself drift to drink his influence
and retrace his disturbed steps—right up to the edge—
but now I pledge to face eternity,

go back to Key West, visit Hemingway's desk,
look past the brevity of his words,
and dance with six-toed cats.

Passageways

Some people navigate dim spaces
of life's caverns
undetected,
leaving no trace
of their passage.

Others carry candles
and torches
that light the way
for privileged travelers
passing by.

True trailblazers use the smoke of their flames
to sign their names on the ceiling—
daring to deface sacred places
to leave proof for future generations
that they, too, passed through.

Fluency

I'm absorbed by the forest
as I take an unfamiliar path and descend
with unseasoned feet; my lumbering body weaves
through branches pointing toward the water.

Concerns ebb as I approach
a hollow trunk—once adrift like me—offering respite
on the river's edge, a place to sit
and sift through ashes of abandoned fire.

Rustling leaves applaud
as I toss simmering deadwood memories
and a desire to wallow in misery
into the sweeping current.

I ascend the trail and flow
with nature's healing breeze.
If I spoke the language of trees, I would know
the word for this budding serenity.

We Look West

Together, from our deck we look west
and applaud each vibrant burst that appears
while the daring sky protests the end of day.

In this stillness of borrowed time,
with cleared calendars,
sharing becomes easier.

After stirring up a bouquet of vintage memories
and floating future plans,
we race twilight to the bottom of the bottle.

Retiring beams kiss the glass lip
of our vital escape from reality
as the sun reluctantly sinks behind the trees.

It's our cue to call it a night,
but we resist the wrap of darkness
because we don't want this moment to fade.

www.ingramcontent.com/pod-product-compliance
Lightning Source LLC
Chambersburg PA
CBHW021239090426
42740CB00006B/599